T0086260

Heartfelt Poems

Poems of the Heart for All

LAURA LLOYD

authorHOUSE®

AuthorHouse™
1663 Liberty Drive
Bloomington, IN 47403
www.authorhouse.com
Phone: 1 (800) 839-8640

© 2016 Laura Lloyd. All rights reserved.

No part of this book may be reproduced, stored in a retrieval system, or
transmitted by any means without the written permission of the author.

Published by AuthorHouse 11/16/2016

ISBN: 978-1-5246-5104-6 (sc)
ISBN: 978-1-5246-5103-9 (e)

Print information available on the last page.

Any people depicted in stock imagery provided by Thinkstock are models,
and such images are being used for illustrative purposes only.
Certain stock imagery © Thinkstock.

This book is printed on acid-free paper.

Because of the dynamic nature of the Internet, any web addresses or
links contained in this book may have changed since publication and
may no longer be valid. The views expressed in this work are solely those
of the author and do not necessarily reflect the views of the publisher,
and the publisher hereby disclaims any responsibility for them.

Dedication

I dedicate this book to my three children, granddaughter "Pebbles", grandson "Little Gordo", belated man Gordo, my man Bobby, my sister Kimberly, my ex Michael (aka Chainz), and my belated Uncle Jack.

I would also like to dedicate this book to my belated Aunt Marilyn, Marilyn Scott. I'd like to thank her for her poems, which I included in this book. I would also like to thank her daughter, Melody, for granting me permission to include them.

This book is also dedicated to those who helped me to get it edited and published as well as to all the other people who have touched my life.

Thank you!

If I Make It

It's been so lonely in my life,
Without my hearts love to hold tight.
Unsure why it happened at all,
But I will miss him for a long while.
If I make it through this pain,
I will not want to love again.
Broken love stabs,
Makes the heart bleed, lungs can't breathe.
It makes tears fall, eyes burn and sting,
Heads hurt, angers rise.
Broken Love has even taken lives.

Perfect Tree

Have you ever seen a perfect tree?
One that grows perfectly, as round as it could be.
It has a straight trunk, no branches to low.
Look at it, with sweet fruit inside.
Is it oranges or apples, that's for you to decide.

My Angels, Don't Have Wings

My angels, they don't have golden wings.
They have no halo, and didn't come
straight from heaven.
But they wear white, they are very nice.
They cared for my weak body, when I was not strong.
They talked to me and made me laugh,
and even help me cut my hair.
My angels, they do not have golden wings
but I bet some day they will.

3

He Could

He could lie to me, like all the others.
Hurt me, by breaking my heart.
But I have a feeling he loves me.
Loves me enough, we will never part.

Gone, But I Have to Carry On

He is gone, in earth he be.
But I have to carry on.
The house is gone; I could not pay.
But I have to carry on.
The life I knew is gone, for good.
But I have to carry on.
For my children, and grandchildren,
I have to carry on.

Relationships of the Heart

Friendships will come and go,
But true love fills your heart,
It is a magical thing to be,
Cause it stays and fills your heart with glee.

Love Is Only Good

Love is only good, if you share it.
That brings kindness into your life,
When you share it with others.
Love is only good, if it is from the heart.
Not just words out of the mouth, or on a letter.
Show the love, by being there, and showing you care.
Love is only good, if you hold it close.
Hold love tight, not loose if it's shared with you.
If you hold it to loose, love may leave you.
Love is only good, if you put your heart and soul into it.
If you put in your all, love will love back.
When it does you'll feel like you're a cloud,
Floating in the breeze in warm spring.

Paint to Picture

A broken heart is like dried up paint.
Sprinkle it with more love, which
will make it flow again.
Paint by number and love,
Has one thing in common,
They both are done in steps, slowly.
Bright pictures make you feel happy inside.
Dark pictures are a sign of sadness.
So from the dried up love paint,
To the soul of the completed picture,
Are the slow steps to take, to make
sure you get it just right.

Secure

All the happiness falls on me, when
I feel secure with thee.
I feel secure,
With your arms around me, holding me tight.
When I see your smile, and twinkle in your eyes.
As I feel your love, and know you're mine.
When I hear your soft words, say I love you.
Because you've made happiness fall on me.

Pets

Pets are wonderful pals to have,
They love you unconditionally.
These wonderful creatures are loyal,
True to you through and through.
Some protect you from any harm,
Some just like to keep your lap warm.
Some work with you, for the law,
Then there are those who work the farm.
But all will be your best friend,
All the way to the end.

You Are My All, My Everything

You're my legs, when I can't walk.
You're my mouth, when I can't talk.
You're my ears, when I can't hear.
You're my eyes, when I can't see.
You're my mind, when I can't think.
You're my energy, when I am weak.
You're my heart, you're my soul.
You are my all, my everything.

11

Happy Birthday, Dear Friend

I wish you all the joy and happiness,
For many years to come.
Wishing you the best of luck,
For this world really sucks.
Hoping for you a great life,
One that takes you far into your dreams.
Hope our friendship lasts forever, and to new heights.
You're the best friend I've ever had, and that's no lie.
So Happy Birthday, Dear Friend.

An Uncle

Today they bury an uncle, I've known most my life.
He is my double-uncle, we're related twice.
This man was a fiery preacher, he
could sing and he could shout
About the word of God, that's what he was about.
But today I will hear someone else say prayer,
Because my loving uncle has gone somewhere.
He has gone to Heaven, forever this will be.
He is with the Lord, Jesus, and Family.
Now my cousins, I know you're sad,
and the tears fill your eyes
But just remember there is a reason why.
His body became weak, though his faith stayed strong.
So my dear uncle had to move on.
Now God will take care of him,
instead of you and friends
But this will not be the end.
Someday your time will come to be
rejoined with your Dad and Mom.

Lost and Found

I lost you once, I cried too hard
My eyes were red, I could not hide
I pained so long, I went numb
So people thought, I was going dumb
I walked like a zombie, I ate like a bird;
I lost 30 pounds, in a month from your love,
I was weak, half starved, and confused,
I could not believe you had left me so soon.
Walking in the sun, but seeing rain.
Laughing out loud, with the hidden pain.
Helping all people I could with no doubt,
While my insides were dying and falling apart.
I'd listen to our favorite song,
Hoping you would come along.
I could not find you in the dark,
But you sure did leave a mark.
For eight months I searched my head,
Trying to figure out why you had fled

Then one day I got online,
I could not believe my hazel eyes.
There, on the page in black and white,
You ask me if I'd take you back.
My heart about leaped out my chest,
My mind it was in protest.
They argued and fused for three or four days,
Then out came the answer my mouth had to say.
Yes I will, my heart wants you so,
But please, this time, don't leave - don't go.

Solitude

I like my solitude on and off,
It usually last three years long.
I close myself up in my room,
Only come out for food and bathroom.
When stress gets too high,
And drama is all I see.
I like my solitude off and on,
Do you see the logic in my insanity?

Fire of the Heart

Nature brings the inter-peace from deep inside me.
In the fall it's the wonder and beauty
of the mountainside.
It's trees full of all colors,
The animals working so hard for slumber.
The winter is full of magic,
White falls to the ground.
Ice forms on trees,
At night it's a world of glistening light.
Now spring, is a world all its own,
Birth is an amazing trick all over the world.

Rain Drop

As I sit here looking at the rain,
I see the drops hit the window and its pane.
I began to wonder,
Do the raindrops feel like me?
Do they feel my pain,
Thrown from its home to be all alone.
Other drops all around it,
But no comfort do they give.
Well I see you raindrop, as your sadness slides,
Leaves a trail of sorrow.
So if there was a way for me,
To take away your agony.
If I could gladden your day,
I would put all effort to make you gay.

Guilt

I lost myself two years ago,
When I lost my one true love of thirty years.
I had lost my soul-mate to a loaded gun.
The guilt I feel cannot be undone,
So for weeks and weeks I try to run.
I was hoping I could lose it, the farther I would go.
But two years later I still feel the guilt,
It floods through me like a raging river in the spring.
Someday I hope the river turns into a brook,
And can relieve me from the large guilt I took.

Joy Will Come

I've lost a lot of loved ones,
From now back to the past.
The people that really made me,
And my soul-mate I do miss.
Loss is hard on the body, mind, and soul,
To the point I want to lose even mine.
Then my mind says logic,
Take time and look around.
There is love for you, all around you,
So happy you should be.
You're sad now, but to lose your life
Is not the way to be.
For your friends, family, and love to be.
Don't make them feel,
So like thee.
To you does come happiness,
But not without the sad.
You've got to make it through this,
Cause I promise joy on the other side.

Rainbow Rain

Today the rain falls, but there's a Rainbow.
Looking over a mountain range, in the misty morning,
There is the biggest Rainbow, I have ever seen.
So now I sit amazed in its beauty,
Wonderful colors all bright and gay.
Wondering if there's an end to its glory,
Or does it fade out till another day.

Staying Here

Being sick with three major illnesses,
Still getting up even with pain.
I'm amazed with people,
That can do that very thing.
The person still smiles and laughs,
At the jokes that they hear.
While the fear inside them screams,
Hey you I am still here.
So to get rid of fear from them and close ones,
If you listen close you will hear them say.
Do not worry I am here to stay.
I'm staying here,
I'm not going anywhere.
This earth does not deserve a break from me,
So I have no plans to leave.
I'm staying right here with you,
Because I'm not done.
I'm going to be the one,
who can beat all three odds.
And I will become,
As strong as I ever was.

Summer Day

After a long hard winter,
But a short Spring.
Summer is here,
To do its thing.
Waking up to the sunrise,
To a warm Summer Day,
Feeling the breeze,
Flowing my way.
The birds are awake,
Singing a sweet tune,
I'm sure they are singing,
Just for me.
A Summer Day spent,
In a field high of grass,
All in the country,
The quite will last.
Up on the porch,
In gram's old rocking chair,
Remembering all the love,
That we shared there.
I wish it was summer,

Could stay year round,
With brooks and springs,
flowing free without care.
Summer days are my favorite memories,
I really like to share,
Cause summer will always come,
Each and every year.
So when you can,
Enjoy a Summer Day,
Make a memory,
For a later day.

Government

The Government says to trust them,
No matter what they do.
But as my age gets higher,
I really do disapprove.
I know of scandals, deceit, and flat out lies.
I'm not a political person,
But it doesn't take one to know the facts.
I'm so this time not enticed to vote,
For one of them right now.
Some try to take our rights away,
Some try to close us off.
To tell you the history of our land,
I know you learned in school,
If it was not for foreigners,
We would not have come to be.
If it was not for all our rights,
There would be chaos in the streets,
Try to take them away and so you shall see.
I know that some need guidance,
That's why the first government made,

The great Constitution for all man to see.
That gave us guidance and rights,
You now try to take from us.
So for the guiders,
We truly have none that we can totally trust.
I believe we need people,
Ones that truly care for us.
not just for the money, or for the fame.
So I think we need to find a way to fill all this space,
With more people like our forefathers,
but not put woman out of place.
All their honesty will maybe fix our country,
So to pull us out of disgrace, and
put us in a better place.

All About Santa

Thanksgiving was here and gone,
And Christmas is on its way.
Wonder what Santa,
Will bring me that day.
To me it's all about Santa,
His reindeer and the sleigh.
The beautiful colors of the lights,
That guide Santa on that night.
Days before Christmas,
People full of glee.
No one thinks of war,
Just peace and harmony.
There is snow upon the ground,
As white as it could be.
Let's go build a snowman,
We can call him Mr. C.
We can name him after Santa,
He would like that I would bet.
I hope he brings me lots of toys,
And lots for all of you.
Cause Santa is giving,
To good boys and girls like you.

We Need to Compromise

When can we find peace,
In a world of violence and deceit?
Where can we find happiness?
When the world is in despair.
I want to know how,
This world turned so cold.
Is it because of politics?
Or maybe just pure hate
We go into war with others, why?
Was it over religion, land, or fame?
No, all this has happened,
Because people can't compromise or agree.

Put Down Your Weapons

I sit here on my bed and listen,
To children outside playing and laughing.
Then the tears roll down my cheeks,
Not because I am sad but because I'm glad.
The noise outside my window,
Is joy and not sorrow.
I know other places, other cities,
Where the sorrow of the children,
Is more than one can bear.
Where guns are shot, bullets flying,
In schools, houses and other buildings.
Parents hide their children; no sun,
no playground, no fun,
For they fear there will be no tomorrow
for their daughters or their sons.

Poems by my belated Aunt Marilyn

The Last Goodbye

I went to see him one last time,
It was against my will.
To see him sleeping all alone,
So quiet and so still.

I did not want to let him go,
But God had other plans.
And though I loved him very much,
I placed him in God's hands.

Now he's gone forever more,
But his memory I will keep.
In my heart I'll see him smile,
And know the peace I seek.

American Hero

The medals tell the story,
Of a hero brave and true.
The Purple Heart the Silver Star,
He fought a war for you.

In service to his nation,
He served his country well.
In battle he was wounded,
But his spirit never fell.

A man who never failed to be,
Right there when trouble brewed.
A willing hand to hold onto,
When heartaches were renewed.

A man so greatly love was he,
By family, friends and all.
Lived his life for you and me,
Then answered God's loving call.

Momma Who Is Santa Claus

Momma who is Santa Claus,
Why don't he come see me.
I've tried so very hard you see,
To be as good as I can be.

I've asked my friends this question,
But they don't seem to know.
So momma who is Santa Claus,
The man that goes Ho! Ho!

I watch for him on Christmas Eve,
To land upon our roof.
I listen for his hearty laugh,
And the sound of a reindeer hoof.

I never get to see him,
Or sit upon his knee.
So momma who is Santa Claus,
Why don't he come see me.

Is it because papa,
Is so very very poor.
That Santa never bothers,
To come around my door.

Please Don't Take My Momma

I was down in Memphis,
In a little vine covered church.
I heard this little girl praying,
Oh how her heart did hurt.

You see her mother was sick in bed,
She thought she would die that day.
And when I walked into that church,
I heard this little girl pray.

Please don't take my momma,
Don't take her away from me.
I am just a blind girl
And you know that I can't see.

So I knelt down beside her,
As she prayed with all her heart.
Please don't take my momma Lord,
For we never more should part.

36

Now momma said if we should pray,
In Jesus Holy name.
He would answer ever prayer,
And so we did the same.

The Lord looked down upon this child,
And touched her mother's brow.
He said your faith has saved her,
Go be with her now.

Little Card

A little card a little treat,
Because I think you're very sweet.
I love you more with passing time,
Won't you be my Valentine.

Blessing

May your day be blessed with sunshine,
And your heart be filled with love.
May blessings fall upon you,
From Heaven up above.

May God's hand be upon you,
To keep you from all harm,
And fill your soul with happiness,
To keep your spirit warm.

Send Him My Way

When I was just a little girl, I met the boy next door.
As we were growing up, I loved him more and more.
Then one day you came along, and
stole his love from me.
You don't love him anymore, but you won't set him free.

Now I won't interfere, with your family and your life.
I am so in love with him, but you are still his wife.
I can't help loving him more and more each day.
So if you don't want him anymore,
just send him my way.

As the years go slowly by you don't seem to care
Just how much you're hurting him, or
the heartaches that he bears.
If you would only let him go, I'd take him back today.
So if you don't want him anymore,
just send him my way.

You run around with other guys, and
you know that's not right.
While he sits alone at home, almost every night.
I'm asking you to set him free, that's all I've got to say.
If you don't want him anymore, just send him my way.

Todd's Poem

Way back in nineteen sixty-four,
I had a baby boy.
He was such a little thing.
He was my pride and joy.

When he was only six year old,
Off to school he went.
In brand new jeans and underwear,
He was quite a gent.

Then next he was a teenager,
Always making trouble.
Today he bought his first car,
And my troubles even double.

One day while I wasn't looking,
He grew to be a man.
Then before I knew it,
I was holding his sons hand.

Grandma's House

If I could be a kid again,
Just for a day or two,
I'd go right over to grandma's house,
And I'll tell you what I would do.

I'd get up at dawn and run to the barn,
I'd feed the chickens and hen.
I'd pet the lamb with the wooly coat,
And visit the pigs in their pen.

I'd play in the hayloft all day long,
With the old hound dog by my side.
I'd search that barn from bottom to top,
To find a good place to hide.

I'd eat my supper by the kerosene lamp,
And read til my eyes were red.
Then I'd climb those stairs two at a time,
And jump in the old feather bed.

Little Note

Someday when I am gone,
They'll find this little note
And know how much I loved them,
With every word I wrote.

To my daughter:
You are the youngest of my children,
And the closest one of all.
Thank you for four beautiful granddaughters,
With them I had a ball.

To my first granddaughter:
You are so very special,
God sent you to ease my pain
Of losing my son so early,
And to give me joy again.

To my second granddaughter:
Your independence is so amazing,
With your grace and all your charm.
Your spirit is awakening,
So gentle and so warm.

To my third granddaughter:
You're a very sweet young girl,
I love you more each day.
You always cuddle in my arms,
In a very special way.

To my fourth granddaughter:
You're just a little baby,
But how I love you so.
I'm glad to be your nanny,
And just wanted you to know.

I love you all.
Nanny

Printed in the United States
by Bookmasters

Printed in the United States
By Bookmasters